I0538615

THE DEMON DRINK

Eighty and more are the years of my life
Never has Alcohol wetted my lips
Though broken with sorrow, though feeble with Pain
Sternly refusing the much-lauded Sips.

Good Goddess of Temperance, tis thee I adore
Thy Hand has upheld me, and still holds me fast
Though short be the Road I may yet have to walk
I promise I'll hold to thy Hand to the last.

From *Octogenarian Teetotallers; with 113 Portraits*
The National Temperance League, 1897

The brow with clammy moisture spread
The febrile pulse, the aching head
The cheeks' pale glow, with wrinkles hid
The bloodless lip, the heavy lid
The reddening eyes' unsteady glance
These are thy marks – *intemperance*!

THE DEMON DRINK

THE VICTORIAN INEBRIATE'S
GUIDE TO THE EVILS OF
ALCOHOL
AND HOW TO ESCAPE THEM

Compiled by 'Abstinens'

Roger Houghton
London

About the Author

Gerard Macdonald is a New Zealander who has lived in Sussex for many years, with his wife, son and daughter. He writes books (including the bestselling *Once a Week is Ample* and *Dear Prudence*) and screenplays; battling always against the twin temptations of public house and gin palace. From this continuing struggle, the present work was born.

First published 1986
© Gerard Macdonald 1986

Set in Linotron Ehrhardt by Gee Graphics
Printed and bound in Great Britain by Mackays of Chatham Ltd
for Roger Houghton Ltd, in association with J. M. Dent and Sons Ltd,
Aldine House, 33 Welbeck Street, London W1M 8LX

British Library Cataloguing in Publication Data

Abstinens
   The demon drink: advice on the awful
   effects of alcohol and how to escape them.
   1. Drinking customs – Anecdotes, facetiae,
   satire, etc.
   Rn: Gerard Macdonald I. Title
   294.1′3′0207   GT 2880

ISBN 1 85203 008 9

Contents

AUTHORITIES QUOTED IN THIS WORK

1. Sir Thomas Barlow: *The Prevailing Intemperance among Women*, London: Church of England Temperance Society, 1902.

2. H. Norman Barnett: *Legal Responsibility of the Drunkard*, London: Baillière Tindall & Cox, 1908.

3. Rev. Dr Lyman Beecher: *Six Sermons on the Nature, Occasions, Signs, Evil and Remedy of Intemperance*, Bradford: T. Inkersley & Co., 1830.

4. Professor G. Bunge: *Alcoholic Poisoning and Degeneration*, London: A. Owen & Co., 1905.

5. William B. Carpenter: *On the Use and Abuse of Alcoholic Liquors*, London: Charles Gilpin, 1850.

6. Dr George B. Cutten: *The Psychology of Alcoholism*, London & Felling-on-Tyne: The Walter Scott Publishing Company, 1907.

7. E. C. Delavan: *Temperance Essays*, New York: The National Temperance Society, 1866.

8. Dr Duncan: *Wholesome Advice against the Abuse of Hot Liquors*, London: H. R. Rhodes, 1706.

9. *Easy Outlines of the Historical Syllabus*, London: Church of England Temperance Society, 1906.

10. Walter N. Edwards: *One Hundred and Seventy-five Temperance Proverbs*, London: Richard J. James, 1907.

11. Walter N. Edwards: *The Red Book: a Vademecum*, London: Richard J. James, 1905.

12. Walter N. Edwards: *Science Chats for Boys and Girls*, London: Charles H. Kelly, 1902.

13. Walter N. Edwards: *The Temperance Compendium*, London: Richard J. James, 1906.

14. Charles H. Follen: *Inebriety*, Edinburgh: Oliphant, Anderson & Ferrier, 1898.

15. R. B. Grindrod: *The Nation's Vice*, London: Hodder & Stoughton, 1884.

16. Dr Sylvanus Harris: *Craving for Drink*, London: S. W. Partridge, 1883.

17. Edward Harwood: *Of Temperance and Intemperance*, London: T. Becket, 1774.

18. Dr C. F. Hodge: *The Influence of Alcohol on Growth and Development*, Boston: Houghton Mifflin, 1903.

19. Sir Victor Horsley and Mary D. Sturge: *Alcohol and the Human Body*, London: Macmillan & Co. Ltd., 1909.

20. Allen Leslie Howard: *7000 Facts about Temperance*, Toronto: William Briggs, 1908.

21. Dr Fred Heman Hubbard: *The Opium Habit and Alcoholism*, New York: A. S. Barnes & Co., 1881.

22. Theo B. Hyslop: *Alcohol and Empire-Building*, London: Church of England Temperance Society, 1906.

23. Rev. H. Jeffreys: *Appeal in Behalf of Temperance*, Bombay: British and Foreign Temperance Society, n/d.

24. William E. Livesey: *Alcohol and Children*, Liverpool: The Booksellers' Company, 1910.

25. Charles Meadows: *My Experience as a Moderate Drinker, a Drunkard, and Total Abstainer*, London: The Literary Society, n/d.

26. Medicus: *Side-lights on Alcohol, and its Action on the Human Organism*, London: The Church of England Temperance Society, n/d.

27. M. Milburn: *Demoralisation and Disappointment the result of the Establishment of Beer-Shops*, London: Houghton and Stoneman, 1849.

28. Rev. William Moister: *The Evil and the Remedy, or the Sin and Folly of Intemperance and the Wisdom and Excellence of Total Abstinence from all Intoxicating Drinks, with observations on the use of Tobacco and other Narcotics*, London: The Weslyan Conference Office, 1877.

29. Samuel Morewood: *An Essay on the Inventions and Customs of both Ancients and Moderns in the Use of Inebriating Liquors*, London: Longman, Hurst, Rees, Orme, Brown and Green, 1824.

30. *Octogenarian Teetotallers, with 113 Portraits*, London: The National Temperance League, 1897.

31. S. Ellen Orme: *Drink and Infantile Mortality*, London: Richard J. James, 1906.

32. Viscount Peel: *Female Intemperance: Is it Increasing?*, London: Church of England Temperance Society, 1849.

33. William Prynne: *Healthe's Sicknesse*, London, 1628.

34. J. T. Rae: *The Alcohol Factor in Social Conditions*, London: P. S. King & Son, 1914.

35. Dr G. Archdall Reid: *Alcoholism, a Study in Heredity*, London: T. Fisher Unwin, 1901.

36. Dr J. James Ridge: *The Temperance Primer*, London: National Temperance League, 1879.

37. Dr J. Starke: *Alcohol*, London: G. P. Putnam's Sons, 1907.

38. *Tracts on Total Abstinence*, Glasgow: Robert J. Brown, n/d.

39. D. W. Turner: *Dirt and Disease*, London, 1884.

40. Dr John Ware: *Remarks on the History and Treatment of Delirium Tremens*, Boston: N. Hale's Steam Power Press, 1831.

41. John Wishart: *Home and Foreign Alcoholic Beverages*, London: Richard J. James, 1906.

42. John Wishart: *Simple Substitutes for Alcohol*, London: Richard J. James, 1906.

43. *Why I am a Rechabite*, London: John Heywood Ltd., 1906.

44. Thomas Young: *England's Bane, or, the Description of Drunkennesse*, London: William Jones, 1617.

1

THE EMBRYONIC ALCOHOLIC

DRUNKEN SPERM ENGENDERS INEBRIATE INFANT –
WRINKLED BABIES SHOW ALCOHOLIC ANCESTRY – INFANT
BORN DRUNK AND LATER DIES – DEATH AND DISEASE
DECIMATE CHILDREN OF DRINKERS

Dear Abstinens
My Baby, in his first year of life, indulges himself recklessly
in Milk. I fear he may do the same with Alcohol; his father
being a sadly indulgent Coal-Whipper.
  Could this man have sewn me with Inebriate Seed?
                              Evils of Drink, Ebury Bridge

Dear Evils
Wedded to a drunken Coal-
Whipper, Madam, only
chastity would save you from
receiving intemperate seed.

In this connection, Mr Walter
Edwards has wisely said 'the body
of the father may be so saturated
with Alcohol that *the drunken sperm
cell* fertilises the ovum in such a
way as to transmit to the Offspring
the tendency to Drunkenness,
*even though the child were begotten in a
sober interval*'.[21]

Though you can scarcely
save the present Suckling, you
would be wise not to extend
your family further.

                    Abstinens

*'transmits to the Offspring the
tendency to Drunkeness'*

9

Dear Abstinens
My Children, some scarcely out of the womb, are uniformly
Small and Wrinkled. Could this be due to the fact that their
Father is a Jockey, and we are neither of us Young?
  Or is it a sign that our Ancestors succumbed to Alcohol?
                                    Litter of Eight, Littlehampton

Dear Litter
The eminent Mr Harwood
suggests that your problem is
an Alcoholic inheritance. This
brings, he says, 'children of
diminutive, pygmy size, who
look old and withered when
they have not yet, alas!
attained the evening of the
first day'.[17]

   I fear that you are seeing
evidence of the Bottle, not the
Jockey.

                        Abstinens

'Children who look old
and withered, when they have not yet
attained the evening of the first day'

Dear Abstinens
My Child, at the age of Two, is still Unsteady on his feet.
Might he have Inherited the evil of Intemperance?
                                    Troubled Mother, Tunbridge Wells

Dear Mother
Does your Infant hold on to Objects for support?
Mr Carpenter writes of such a boy 'who *was born drunk*
and seen, at a very tender age, quite Intoxicated, and
clinging for support to a Lamp-post. He was never known

to be perfectly Sober, and died at the age of eighteen, of Alcoholic Degeneration'.[52]

If I were you, I should enjoy your Offspring while you can.

Abstinens

Dear Abstinens
My Wife and I have taken the occasional glass of Stout, though now no longer, since recently joining the Order of Rechabites.

Will this past Weakness injure our numerous Offspring?
An Erstwhile Toper, Tottenham

Dear Toper
Dr Cutten has examined 57 children of drunkards like yourself. Twenty-five, he writes, 'died soon after birth. Of the remainder, six were Idiots, five Dwarfs, five Epileptics, one each had Chorea, chronic Hydrocephalus, Hare Lip and Club Foot; while *two of the Epileptics became Alcoholics*.'[6]

You can, at the least, look forward to a certain variety in your issue.

Abstinens

'two of the Epileptics became Alcoholics'

2

YOUTHFUL TOPERS

HORROR OF UNDERSIZED INEBRIATES – GIN FATAL FOR
THREE-YEAR-OLDS – MONIED INFANTS IN DANGER – NOT
EVEN THE SABBATH SAFE – SMALL BEER AND ANIMAL
PASSIONS

Dear Abstinens
I now notice infant Inebriates scattered like Dogs about the
floor of the local Gin Palace. Is this, Sir, a Recent
development?

Colonel Sir R. E. J., Blackheath

Dear Colonel
Professor Bunge writes of a woman 'who used to go to
the Public-house at such an age *that she could not even*
walk down the steps . . . but had to sit down and wriggle
with the bottle in her arms'.[4]

Clearly, the infant Inebriate has been with us for
some while.

Abstinens

'the infant Inebriate
has been with
us for some while'

Dear Abstinens
My Nursling has emptied the dregs of a Glass, left by his
unregenerate Father.

Do you suppose he will survive? Or has the Drink a hold
on him?

Tormented Young Mother, Truro

Dear Tormented

It is not clear whether you are concerned about the
survival of your husband or your child. If the child, Miss
Ellen Orme suggests that his chances are slim.

In a similar case, Miss Orme writes of a three-year-
old 'creeping downstairs to get a sip of Gin or Whiskey.
It was found by its Grandfather, but not in time to save
it from the fatal Drink, for it had convulsions and
Died.'[31]

I trust that this, though not Optimistic, is what you
wanted to know.

Abstinens

'creeping downstairs to get a sip of
Gin or Whiskey'

13

Dear Abstinens
Having read of the infant Inebriate, I wonder if I am well
advised to give my Child his mite of money for Lunch. May
the little Creature not waste it on Whiskey or Gin?
                                    Paterfamilias, Witley

Dear Paterfamilias
You could do no better than follow the Reverend Dr
Lyman Beecher, who writes, 'I never give permission for
an infant to go out, or give a pittance of money to be
expended for his gratification, unattended by an earnest
injunction not to drink ardent spirits, or any inebriating
liquor'.[3]

   Such Instruction will make any Infant neglect his
neighbourhood Gin Palace.

                                              Abstinens

Dear Abstinens
I would not send my Child out unattended save to a Sunday
School. Your readers are advised to do the same, should they
wish their Issue to tread in the paths of righteousness.
                                 Sabbatarian, East Sowerby

Dear Sabbatarian
Not even the Sunday School is proof against the bottle.
The Reverend William Moister tells of Sunday scholars,
fallen so low through drink, 'that they have been found
on the Sabbath evening, in miserable dancing rooms,
actually singing the hymns they had learned at school for the
amusement of their dissipated and wicked companions'.[28]

   You might do well, Sir, to see how your son spends
his Sundays.

                                              Abstinens

Dear Abstinens
My heir is at a School which serves Small Beer with the
Pupils' evening repast. Surely such mild Licentiousness will
not harm the lad?

Sussex Squire

Dear Squire
Much depends upon your point of view.

According to Mr Livesey, 'alcohol taken during
school life interferes with the rapid development of the
brain. Its use produces inability to do school work
satisfactorily. Later on in life, the poorly developed
brain cells mean defective mental power, weakened self
control, *the excitement of animal passions* and the
perversion of thoughts and ideas prone to lead to
depraved habits and immorality.'[23]

Perhaps, though, you attach some other meaning to
the notion of harm?

Abstinens

'a School which serves Small Beer with the Pupils' evening repast'

3

THE LUSTFUL INEBRIATE

STOCKBROKER BUYS VERMINOUS WOMAN – ALCOHOL
CAUSE OF UNMENTIONABLE DISEASE – DRINK MAKES MAN
HOT AND FECUND

Dear Abstinens
I have recently seen my Fiancé (a Stockbroker) in the
company of an unfortunate young person. She was notably
Unclean; and both of them, I fear, seemed Less than Sober.
Is this distressing lapse likely to recur?

Miss Adelaide F., Epsom

Dear Adelaide
Recur it will, unless your betrothed has recently taken
the pledge.

Mr Edward Harwood tells us that 'young men in a
state of inebriety, hesitate not to throw themselves into
the arms of the very Lowest class of Woman – creatures
covered with Filth, Itch and Rags, devoured with
Vermin, whom in their senses and Sober hours they
would have regarded with the utmost Detestation and
Horror'.[17]

You might check that your loved one does have these
Penitent feelings; and that he retains about his person
no living relics of his Lapse.

Abstinens

'no living relics of his Lapse'

'Both, I fear, seemed Less than sober'

Dear Abstinens
A close friend of mine, in a moment of weakness, has taken to Drink. Now he suspects he may have contracted Something Unmentionable, namely Syphilis.

Is it possible that Alcohol might cause this loathsome Disease?

Patient's Friend, Eppingham

Dear Patience
Mr McAdam Eccles writes, 'I ask every man infected with Syphilis *what condition he was in at the time he caught it*. I have been astonished at the number who were under the influence of alcohol at the time.'[34] To which the eminent Sir Victor Horsley adds, 'A great number of individuals become infected with Venereal Disease *simply because they are intoxicated*.'[34]

No doubt Alcohol is the proximate cause of this noxious complaint. But your Friend might also do well to avoid Promiscuous Sex.

Abstinens

17

Dear Abstinens
I am ashamed to say that the Demon Drink has the Intimate
Effect of making my person Hot; and of leading me
shamefully to Sensual Excess.

Is there, I wonder, some Connection between Carnality,
Heat and Drink?

Heat of the Moment, Haslemere

Dear Heat
Dr Duncan confirms that Liquor does indeed make
creatures Hot; and this Heat engenders dangerous
degrees of Lust.

Beasts, says Dr Duncan, 'seldom couple but in Hot
seasons. A cat is the only four-footed creature that
begins in *February*, because it is a *very Hot creature*. The
vigour of the Male kind, and the Fecundity of both
Sexes, are Certainly the effects of *Heat*.'[8]

In the light of this, Sir, you would be well advised to
forgo Alcohol entirely. Failing that, you might try
Tippling in a Stone Cold Bath.

Abstinens

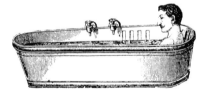

'you might try Tippling in a Stone Cold Bath'

4

THE WINE-BIBBING WOMAN

EXECUTION OF WOMAN CURES ALCOHOL HABIT – FALLEN
FEMALE SELLS TEETH FOR DRINK – LADY EATS OUNCES OF
OPIUM – SCOTS CONVICTED: DRUNK IN CHARGE OF
CHILD – PREGNANCY MAKES ALCOHOLIC MOTHER PAWN
POSSESSIONS – DRUNK AT THE GROCER'S

Dear Abstinens
My Husband recommends the Capital Sanction for Female
Drinkers. It is not my custom to Disagree with the Head of
the Household, but this does seem a little harsh.
*   Are there precedents for such Penalties?*

*   Temperate Wife, Torquay*

Dear Temperate
In this connection, there
are impeccable precedents.

The Reverend William
Moister, writing of Rome,
says that 'wine was
forbidden to women, *lest by
its use they should fall into
some extravagances*. On
conviction, the guilty
woman received the same
punishment as if she had
committed adultery, *which
was nothing less than
death*'.[28]

*'My Husband recommends
the capital Sanction for
Female Drinkers.'*

It is difficult to imagine a more effective way of
ending Female Insobriety.   Abstinens

Dear Abstinens
I notice a number of toothless Fallen Women frequenting the Gin Palace.

As an Observer of Mankind, this interests me. Do Female Topers commonly lose their Teeth?

Tooth and Nail, Fulham

Dear Tooth
The loss is not, I fear, fortuitous. Dr Sylvanus Harris describes a lady dipsomaniac 'who had nearly all her teeth extracted, and sold them for the purpose of gratifying her craving for intoxicants'.[16]

The mind recoils from the thought of what these Tormented Souls may have to sell for their second round of drinks.

Abstinens

Dear Abstinens
To divert my mother from Drinking, our doctor has recommended Opium.

Is this, in your view, a wise alternative?

Seed of the Poppy, South Wimbledon

Dear Poppy
Much depends on whether you want an Alcohol Addict or an Opium Addict in the family.

Mr Morewood offers the case of a lady 'prevented by her friends from Excessive Indulgence in ardent Spirits, who substituted Opium; and from its constant use can now swallow an Ounce *with as much ease and indifference as a Boy would swallow a Liquorice Ball!*'.[29]

Abstinens

Dear Abstinens
As one who knows several weak-willed Mothers, I wonder
whether these Women commit any Criminal offence when
they have taken their glasses of Wine?
                              Reverend W. M., Rottingdean

Dear Reverend
Indeed they do. To take only one example, Mr Allen
Leslie Howard tells us (in his Seven Thousand Facts
about Temperance) that 'over a hundred women were
recently convicted in Edinburgh of being *drunk in charge
of a Child*'.[19]

I trust, Sir, this may sober the dissolute Parents of
your Parish.

                                              Abstinens

'convicted of being drunk in charge of a Child'

Dear Abstinens
Though fond of an occasional glass of Porter, I fear it may
atrophy my ovaries.
  Can you let me know whether this is the case?
                              Doubtful Governess, Abergavenny

Dear Doubtful
That awful consequence is more than likely: it is
certain.

  Dr Cutten tells us that, in women given to Alcohol,
'menstruation ceases prematurely and the Ovaries
atrophy'.[6]

  You can, at least, take comfort in the fact Nature no
longer allows you Offspring. Your innocent Issue would
otherwise inherit the Vice.

                                                  Abstinens

Dear Abstinens
My wife – who is both Pregnant and Inebriate – has taken to
Pawning our Possessions.
  Is such Profligacy common in these cases?
                              Distracted Curate, Cuckfield

Dear Distracted
Your Wife's recklessness is far from Unique. To take
but one instance, Dr Sylvanus Harris tells of a woman
who 'when quickening with each of her Children, was
afflicted with a craving for stimulants to a Dreadful
Extent. She several times broke up the Home, *pawning*
and selling everything she could lay her hands upon in order
to procure Intoxicants.'[16]

  In these circumstances, you must calculate carefully
how many Infants you can afford. If it be any
consolation, Dr Harris concludes that his lost soul 'has
now ceased Childbearing, and is a perfectly sober,
discreet, temperate Lady'.

                                                  Abstinens

Dear Abstinens

My young wife runs up uncommonly large bills for Earl Grey at the Grocer's Shop. Since we Eat and Drink abstemiously, this is hard to explain.

Do you suppose that my Spouse may be Sipping something Stronger than Tea?

Uneasy Husband, Ullswater

Dear Uneasy

The learned Professor Bunge quotes a Mrs Hawkes, of Bristol, 'who brought a very heavy charge against Grocers' Shops. She was *convinced* that a great quantity of so-called Groceries – butter, tea and so on – *were only other names for Alcohol*'. The Professor adds that this sort of thing 'greatly increases the Consumption of Alcohol in the homes of the Poorer Classes'.[4]

You may find, Sir, that your feckless lady has indeed been buying her Earl Grey in bottles.

Abstinens

'Do you suppose my Spouse may be Sipping something Stronger than Tea?'

5

THE DEVOUT DRINKER

IS GOD TEETOTAL? – MILLIONS OF DRUNKEN ANGELS IN
DELIRIUM TREMENS – SCROFULOUS DAUGHTER OF VICAR
DROWNS IN RUM – GOD NOT RESPONSIBLE FOR
ALCOHOL – REFORMED DRUNKARD SEDUCED BY
COMMUNION WINE – CLERGYMAN WITH KNIFE ATTACKS
CONSTABLE

Dear Abstinens
I assume God is a Teetotaller?

Sword of Flame, Surrey

Dear Sword
In this respect, Sir, God is as pure as You or I.
   The Church of England Temperance Society has
confirmed that 'the stories of the Rechabites, St John
the Baptist, Samuel, et cetera, show *that God approves of
Total Abstinence*'.[9]

Abstinens

Dear Abstinens
I am sorry to bother you again, but what of the Angels?
Can we be certain they too are Abstainers?

Sword of Flame, Surrey

Dear Sword,
With Angels, unfortunately, we are on much more shaky
ground. Indeed, the Reverend Moister asserts that there
are '*millions* of drunken Angels in the Lower Heavens,
who are still Dwelling in a state of Delirium Tremens, and
have not power to regain control of their own souls'.[28]
   I can only suggest that Non-Drinkers should aim, in
any Future Life, for one of Heaven's higher Eyries.

Abstinens

*'there are millions
of drunken Angels'*

Dear Abstinens
*As a Man of the Cloth, I assume that my Offspring – who
are yet in the Nursery – will scarcely Stray from the Path of
Righteousness?*

Minister of our Lord, Paddington

Dear Minister of our Lord
Does the Scripture not
say that the Righteous
will be Cast Down?

Dr Harris tells us, in
this connection, of the
Vicar 'who brought up his
son for the Ministry. In
spite of the Moral Checks
which his Office imposed
on his appetites, the son
*drank the Sacramental
Wine*, and went Drunk
into the Pulpit.' In this
same unfortunate family,
'the eldest daughter
tapped a barrel of rum,
and was discovered dead

*'the son drank the
Sacramental Wine'*

under it; while the second daughter, who suffered from Scrofula, also died in the midst of a Drunken Paroxysm'.[16]

You will recall, Sir, Deuteronomy xxxii. 33: 'Their wine is the poison of dragons, and the cruel venom of asps'.

Abstinens

Dear Abstinens
Is God responsible for the Evil of Alcohol?
Troubled in Faith, Birmingham

Dear Troubled in Faith
Dr Ridge, on the whole, thinks not. Our Gracious Father, he says, 'will not leave the Ferment of the Grape to intoxicate us. He will go on to change the poisonous Alcohol into harmless and useful Vinegar.' It is *Men*, adds Dr Ridge, 'who take a great deal of trouble to prevent His doing this, and ought not to charge Him with sending Wine and Spirits to tempt and injure the Creatures He has made'.[35]

Abstinens

Dear Abstinens
As one who has been a Lost Soul and a Drunkard, I fear to taste the Communion Wine. Am I wise to refuse this Sacrament?
Reclaimed from the Pit, Putney

Dear Reclaimed
It is hard to criticise your decision. There are many examples of the Dangers of the Sacrament. We read, for example, of a reclaimed Drunkard who did no more than taste Communion Wine. 'The same day, a Sunday, *he was taken up by the Police for beating his wife*, in a state of Mad Drunkenness.'[38] Yet another ex-toper drank

Communion Wine' – and he, *who seemed a Saint*, went home, got Drunk, and died a Drunkard'.[7]

A third writes that 'the smell of Communion wine roused his Long-Sleeping Desire for Alcoholic Drink. The fearful Temptation was such that *he has never since dared to attend Communion.*'[38]

Abstinens

Dear Abstinens
The Vicar of our Parish is often Unsteady on his Feet, as if he had indulged in Drink. Is this possible, in a Man of God?
Perplexed Parishioner, Muddles Green

Dear Perplexed
Sad to say, even God's Chosen can Stumble.

The Reverend Moister records a drunken Clergyman of Elmstead, Essex, who 'followed a Police Constable *and struck him a violent blow on the left side of the head.* The Constable called for assistance, and, two other persons coming up, the Reverend Gentleman, *who had a large table knife upon him*, was overpowered.'[27]

You would do well, Sir, to have a Quiet Word with your Spiritual Mentor, at a time when you are sure he is Unarmed.

Abstinens

'followed a Police Constable and struck him a violent blow'

6

THE AGED IMBIBER

Dear Abstinens
Is it possible for the Aged to Catch Light and Burn?
                    Mysteriously Bereaved, West Midlands

Dear Bereaved
Spontaneous Combustion is rare at any age. Exactly
how did your Bereavement occur?

                                        Abstinens

Dear Abstinens
My Grandfather, who was both Overweight and Alcoholic,
suddenly took fire. We were Unprepared since, to my memory,
he never Burned before.
    Grandfather was, I fear, quite reduced to Ash by the time
we Extinguished him.
                    Mysteriously Bereaved, West Midlands

Dear Bereaved
These Details shed a very different light on the
Combustion of your Forebear.
    Mr William Carpenter writes of many similar cases
'where the body of the Drunkard takes fire very rapidly,
and burns as if it were highly Inflammable'.
    The greater number of recorded instances, he adds,
'*occurred among Fat Old People who had been Spirit*
Drinkers'.[5]

28

If you have other aged relatives in the same condition, I can only suggest you keep them well away from Candles.

Abstinens

Dear Abstinens
My Aunt, who is an Unobtrusive Drinker, has scarcely moved for a month; except for her Eyes, which follow you round the room.

Do you suppose this is due to Laziness, Lethargy, or some more serious Affliction?

Uneasy Nephew, Littlehampton

'her Eyes follow you round the Room'

Dear Uneasy
It may be that your Aunt has simply positioned herself beside the tantalus, and has no inclination to move. On the other hand, she may be paralysed. According to Mr Norman Barnett, 'in females who are quiet, steady tipplers, there is paralysis, usually of the legs, from the knee down, and of the feet'.[2]

If your Aunt is still in the same place next month, choose a time when she has no Glass in her hand, and give her Knees a sharp knock. You will soon learn whether the lady is Lethargic, or simply Unable to Move.

Abstinens

'on the other hand, she may be paralysed'

Dear Abstinens
My elderly Professor of Theology, a man of somewhat Hirsute appearance, now interrupts his Lectures with a constant Scratching and Snarling.

Could it be that Mr Darwin is correct in his Account of our Ancestry?

Discipulus Dubius, Cantabriensis

Dear Dubius
What you describe has nothing to do with Mr Darwin or, indeed, the Book of Genesis; it is a condition of the Old and Inebriated.

Speaking of Elderly Alcoholics, the learned Dr

Carpenter says that 'they are liable to an Eruption all over their bodies, which is attended with a very Afflicting Itching, and which they Propagate from One part of their bodies to Another, with their own Nails, by Scratching themselves'.[5]

Let your Professor of Theology, Discipulus, consider Deuteronomy xxi: He is a Glutton and a Drunkard, and all the men of his City shall stone him with stones that he die.

Abstinens

'a man of somewhat Hirsute appearance'

Dear Abstinens
I am compelled to Write with a Delicate Question.
As a man now in Middle Age, and by no means an Abstainer, I must ask whether Alcohol might affect the Male Fertility?

Seed of Onan, Colchester

Dear Seed
There can be no doubt that your Habits have made you Barren; nor that the Fruit of Abstention is Fecundity.

To take but one example, Mr James Clark, of Street, writes that 'he has *no less than fifty-eight* who call him Father and Grandfather, *and not one of them has been contaminated by Alcoholic Liquor*'.[30]

If you wish, Sir, to Continue your Line, I suggest that you Discontinue your Drinking.

Abstinens

7

THE ALCOHOLIC ALIEN

AMERICAN RACE DESTROYED BY DRINK – ABANDONING
SPRINGS OF NATIVE COUNTRY – ALSO SINEWY ABORIGINES
OF CANADA AND FIGHTING KAFFIR – HINDOOS LOSING
THEIR ONLY VIRTUE – UNCIVILISED SWEDES DRINK JUICE
OF ANT

Dear Abstinens
I am considering Marriage to a young American gentleman.
    Since I myself am a member of the Band of Hope, I am
anxious to know whether my Betrothed is likely to indulge in
Wine which Scripture describes as the Poison of Dragons, and
the cruel Venom of Asps (Deut.xxxii.33).

                                        Unsullied, Birmingham

Dear Unsullied
You are, I fear, unlikely to Marry an abstaining
American.
    'The wild American in his native Forests, contented
while he drank the Springs of his country,' writes Dr
Starke, 'has reason to Curse the Day that the English
foreigner brought him Strong Drink which has
debauched his Mind, destroyed his Body, and nearly
extinguished his Race.'[36]
    You would be wise to find out first whether your
American sticks to his Springs; or whether he has
learned, sadly, to seek something Stronger.

                                        Abstinens

Dear Abstinens
I can be persuaded of the Alcoholic American – but what of
the fighting Kaffir, the wild race of Australia, and the sinewy
Aborigine of Canada?
  Will you say, Sir, that these too are Degraded by Drink?
                    Maj.Gen.R.K.S. (Ret), Torquay

Dear Major General (Ret)
It is not I who assert it, but the respected Mr Wishart
and the learned Dr Starke.
   Mr Wishart, indeed, confirms your worst Fears: 'the
wild races of Australia, the fighting Kaffirs, the debased
Hottentots, effeminate Singalese, and the sinewy
Aborigines of Canada – the Anglo-Saxon race *has
polluted them all with Drink*'.[41]

                                    Abstinens

'the effeminate Singalese'

Dear Abstinens
Following your letter on the Abasement of the American race,
I am impelled to ask: Is the Same true of the Hindoo?
Missionary Spirit, Eastbourne

Dear Missionary
Would that it were not. But Dr Starke writes that 'the Hindoos are fast losing the principal, *perhaps the only*, virtue which adorned their character – *the virtue of temperance*'.[37]

Abstinens

Dear Abstinens
I have heard that the Swede drinks the Juice of the Ant. Is this so, or is it a Slander on the Scandinavians?
Surely no Englishman would wish to Drink an Insect?
A Disgusted Patriot, Worthing

Dear Disgusted
The Aperitif you have in mind is not undiluted Ant.

According to Mr Morewood, Swedish brandy is 'enriched with a large Species of Black Ant, which gives the Drink flavour and potency'.[29]

But you are quite right to doubt that the ingestion of Insects will ever Appeal to the English.

Abstinens

8

LOWER–CLASS CRAPULENCE

INEBRIATE WORKER RESEMBLES RHINOCEROS – BOTH PART
OF GOD'S MYSTERIOUS PLAN – DRUNKARDS LESS COMMON
IN CLERGY THAN BUTTON–MAKERS – LOWER–CLASS
LUNATICS PRONE TO INTEMPERANCE – NORTH EUROPEANS
MORE DRUNK THAN THOSE IN THE SOUTH – BOTH LESS
DRUNK THAN SAVAGES

Dear Abstinens
I notice, from the windows of my Hansom, a Degenerate type
of Drinker. Is this, as I suppose, the sad sum of Depraved
Generations whose Inebriate Decline offers a Melancholy
Demonstration of Mr Darwin's speculations?
Theory of Evolution, St James

Dear Theory
Mr Charles H. Follen, for one, supports your view. He
describes the brutal criminal Inebriate of our Cities as
'the blackguard Drunkard of the streets, Low of Brow
and Dark of Visage, born of the Gutters. His sensations
are as quiescent as in a Rhinoceros and are excited only
through the Stomach.

'low of Brow and
Dark of Visage'

'part of God's plan'

He is the Concentrated Living Spawn of the accumulating Growth of Generations into Depravity.'[14]

No doubt such Persons are part of God's plan; as is the Rhinoceros himself. We may not, of course, easily perceive the purpose He has in Mind for either of them.

Abstinens

Dear Abstinens
I write to you as a young girl in love with a Button-Maker.
Mama says that I should marry a better class of person, and has in mind a Medical Man.

Is it true that I shall suffer if I marry Beneath me?
Faltering Fiancée, Oxford

Dear Faltering
You will certainly suffer if you marry a poorer class of Person; and most of all a Button-Maker. Dr Sylvanus Harris has calculated that *one Button-Maker in every 7.2 is a Drunkard*, while only one Medical Man in every 68.3 has the same sad Tendency.[16]

You would, in fact, do even better to Marry a man of the Cloth, should he be available. Among the Clergy *only one in four hundred and seventeen* takes to the Bottle. It is difficult, in these Times, to do better than that.

Abstinens

Dear Abstinens

We are seeking an Asylum in which to house our Mother, the Dowager Baroness. She is, to say the least, Unstable of Mind.

However, we are concerned about the company Mama will keep. I assume that the better Institutions no longer lodge an Intemperate class of Lunatic?

J.deLisle F., Bart, Suffolk

Dear Bart
You are right in thinking that there is a Hierarchy, even among the Unhinged.

In Pauper Lunatic Asylums, according to Mr Carpenter, 'the proportion of those *who have become Insane through Intemperance* is much higher than it is in Asylums *for the reception of Lunatics from the Higher Classes*'.[5]

I have no doubt your Mother will find an Asylum where she enjoys, so far as she may, the remaining years of her Madness.

Abstinens

Dear Abstinens
I am considering a Vacation in Northern Europe, but fear to find the lower classes intemperate.

Are they, as Rumour has it, more Crapulous than the Poor of the South?

A Timid Traveller, Torquay

Dear Timid
Your fears, unfortunately, are well founded. The North Europeans are, according to Dr Archdall Reid, *much more drunken than South Europeans*.

You may find it consoling to know, however, that even the lower orders of Northern Europe are Less drunken than Savages.[35]

Abstinens

9

THE DEGENERATE DIPSOMANIAC

HAIR-TONIC TIPPLER – A PATHOLOGICAL DRINKER –
SUDDEN EXTRUSION OF FUR-COVERED TONGUE – WOMAN
WREATHED WITH RATS – BURNING WIFE IN INTERCOURSE
WITH FELLOW WORKER – BUTTON-MAKER'S EXTREME
REMEDY FOR LOATHSOME CREATURE IN BED

Dear Abstinens
Bottles of Bay Rum keep
disappearing from my Chemist's
Shop. Do you suppose the
Assistant (an Intemperate Young
Man) could possibly be Tippling
with Hair Tonic?
*   Distracted Dispenser, Camden*

'bottles of Bay Rum keep disappearing'

Dear Distracted
What you suggest is More than Possible. To take one
similar Instance, Dr Harris records a Hospital
Attendant who '– when unable to Obtain anything else –
would drink the Alcohol *from bottles containing Human*
pathological Specimens'.[16]
    Such, Sir, is the Craving for Drink.

Abstinens

*'he would drink the Alcohol from bottles containing
Human pathological Specimens'*

Dear Abstinens
My Husband has taken to suddenly Poking out his Tongue,
which is covered with Thick Fur.
   Is this Usual – or are we seeing the Awful Effect of
Indulgence in Alcohol?

Wifely Concern, Colchester

Dear Wifely
Almost certainly the Second, and not the First.
   Dr Ware remarks that, preceding delirium tremens,
'the Tongue is covered with a thin white fur; *more rarely*
with a thick. When asked to show his Tongue, the
drunkard thrusts it out suddenly, with a staring
expression of the eyes.'[40]
   In the light of this Prognosis, it may be that your
Husband has other, and perhaps terminal, Surprises in
store for you.

Abstinens

Dear Abstinens

My Husband bangs into things a lot, for instance, Wardrobes and Walls.

If you ask me, our Albert walks into Walls because he is Drunk, but Albert says No, in fact he Drinks because his Head hurts.

Please let me know which of us is right.

Wondering Wife, West Bromwich

Dear Wondering

Even without the Alcohol, your Husband would be Confused by his Repeated Concussions. But as to Causation, your Albert has some learned support. Mr Charles Follen says that head injuries hold an important place among the causes of Alcoholism. 'Among 123 inebriates, *one in six received Blows to the Head*, and forty-one had Fractures of the Skull.'[14]

Whatever the first cause, you are safe in assuming that while your Husband continues to drink, he will continue to fracture his skull; and while he continues to fracture his skull, he is unlikely to abate his Alcoholism.

Write again if you have any further queries.

Abstinens

Dear Abstinens

I have recently Witnessed my Wife in Lewd Conjunction with my Fellow Workers. She was on fire at the time, and Wreathed with Rats.

Could this Vision be due to Drink?

Hair of the Dog, Dulwich

Dear Hair

What you see is almost certainly due to Drink. The Reverend Moister records the similar case of a Toper 'who saw Devils, Eels and Rats, shook Worms from the ends of his fingers, thought his Bed was on Fire, and saw his wife in Intercourse with his Fellow Workers'.[28]

However, should you find your Wife with child, you may well seek some other Explanation.

Abstinens

Dear Abstinens
My Husband – a good man, but a Button-Maker – has recently taken his life. Suicide apart, his only fault was a constant searching for Serpents.

Would you think Alfred's fatal decision was due to Disillusion with Life, or just to the amount that he Drank?

Bereft, Aberystwyth

Dear Bereft
In the Nature of the Case, we shall never now know. But Authorities record many working men 'who imagine themselves in Bed, environed with Serpents and other Loathsome Creatures, and who not infrequently commit Suicide in their efforts to escape from these Horrors'.[12]

If your late Husband ever imagined a Loathsome Creature on his Bed, aside of course from yourself, then I fear that your question is answered.

Abstinens

'he imagined a Loathsome Creature on his bed'

10

THE INSANE ALCOHOLIC

COMPANY IN ASYLUM NO BETTER THAN GIN PALACE –
MIDDLE-AGED SON TAKES ROAD TO INSANITY, CRIME,
SENSUALITIES, INCENDIARISM AND MURDER – WOMEN AS
PRONE TO ALCOHOLIC INSANITY AS MEN

Dear Abstinens
I am pleased to say that my Cousin, an unrepentant Imbiber,
has recently been committed to an Insane Asylum.
There, I imagine, he will have Leisure to consider God's
Mercy, and be in a better class of Company than was
customary at the Gin Palace.

Faith and Hope, Felixstowe

Dear Faith
Laudable as your sentiments are, I should not be too
confident. According to Dr Heman Hubbard,
Alcoholics are easily influenced 'and the Persons they
are thrown into contact with at an Asylum *are just as*
Bad, if not worse, than their Companions at home'.[21]

Abstinens

'persons at an
Asylum are just
as Bad . . . as
their Companions'

Dear Abstinens

My Son, at the age of forty, has recently started to Drink,
and I imagine that liquor will make him a Lunatic.
I trust you will tell me this Fear is Unfounded?

Mater Dolorosa, Balham

Dear Mater

Would that I could set your mind at rest; but it cannot
be.

Mr Edwards tells us that Spirituous Liquors 'excite
almost invariably a Demon-like Frenzy, and when thus
Intoxicated people become capable of any Imaginable
Infamy or Crime . . . the whole hydra Evil *culminates in*
Idiocy, Insanity, and commission of all kinds of Crimes and
Sensualities; Theft, Incendiarism, Suicide and Murder'.[11]

I have no wish to interfere in your family life, but
might it not be simpler if your Son signed the pledge?

Abstinens

Dear Abstinens

Unfortunately, I number among my Friends several Men who
have become Insane through Alcohol. Are Women similarly
afflicted, or is Insanity simply the Achilles' Heel of the
Stronger Sex?

Impartial Observer, Isfield

'she fell into a tub of hot water and was scalded to death'

43

Dear Observer

On this subject, the Reverend Moister writes of a drunken Liverpool woman 'who fell into a tub of hot water and was scalded to death; of a female who, fighting when Drunk, received a Blow of which she died; another Female when Tipsy jumped out of a window and was killed; while yet another, when Drunk, hanged herself '.[28]

You, Sir, must judge whether these are the Actions of Rational and Sober Ladies.

Abstinens

'received a Blow of which she died'

11

DEALERS IN DRINK

PUBLICANS COMPARED TO RATTLESNAKES – NEED TO BE
KILLED OR BOXED UP – REFINED PERSONS NOT FOUND IN
PUBLIC HOUSES – FORNICATION AND BAD LANGUAGE
MORE LIKELY

Dear Abstinens
I have led a Blameless Life, up to my present age, and run a
respectable Public House, yet was recently denounced as a
Rattlesnake. This unjust appellation has given me great pain,
and made me consider a new trade, for example, clergyman or
shoemaker.

Perplexed Publican, Balls Pond

Dear Perplexed
Whether justly or not, Publicans are often seen as
members of the Snake family. We need look no further
than Mr Harwood, who writes that *there are no half-way*
measures in dealing with Mad Dogs or Rattlesnakes. 'Unless
they are Killed or Boxed Up, they will kill us. Equally so
it is with those that Manufacture and Sell intoxicating
Liquors.'[17]

Your choice of an alternative trade, incidentally, may
help to lengthen your life. Mr Harwood tells us that the
death rate among dealers in drink is five times as great
as among clergymen, *and six times as great as among*
shoemakers.

More power, Sir, to your last.

Abstinens

Dear Abstinens
My Husband, who visits
Public Houses, says they are
Frequented by the nicest type
of Toper. Others, however,
say that my Oscar will be
led to Blaspheme and
Fornicate with Loose
Women.

   Whom, then, should
I believe?
Mrs Adelaide F.J.,
Amherst

Dear Adelaide
The evidence, I fear,
does little to support your
Spouse. Dr Ridge, to take
only one Witness, writes
that 'drinking leads men
into Bad Company; *and*
bad men and women, when
they begin to Drink, are
sure to use Bad Language
and commit Sin'.[36]

   You might do well, in
the circumstances, to
explore your Husband's
notion of Niceness.

                    Abstinens

'the nicest type of Toper'

46

12

THE SOT AND HIS SPOUSE

WIFE'S DRINKING NOT ADDICTION – SIMPLY AND PURELY
VICIOUS – WOMEN DESIRE DRINK NO MORE THAN
TOBACCO – MARRIAGE AND ALCOHOL LEAD TO AWFUL END

Dear Abstinens
Though an Abstainer myself, I have noticed my Wife –
assuming herself Unobserved – sampling small Glasses of
Wine. This, I am told, marks her as an Alcoholic Woman.
For myself, I prefer to imagine it no more than the native
Viciousness of her Character.

Innocent Adam, Eden Vale

Dear Innocent
Do not despair: most likely your Wife is just morally
degenerate. In his book *Craving for Drink*, Dr Sylvanus
Harris asserts that 'so long as woman retains her
control over the Alcoholic Habit, *her Drinking is Simply
and Purely Vicious'*.[16]

I hope you find this some consolation, Sir, in dealing
with your errant Eve.

Abstinens

'I have noticed my Wife sampling small Glasses of Wine'

47

Dear Abstinens
The moment I was Married, I took the natural step of
forbidding my wife to drink Alcohol.

Since the Evil Fluid has not passed her Lips, I assume that
she will never now desire it?

Master of the House, Macclesfield

Dear Master
Here you have the support of the respected Dr Ridge;
he writes that 'Women who never take Alcoholic Drinks
never miss them – any more than Women desire to
smoke Tobacco, or an Englishman wishes to smoke
Opium.'[36]

Abstinens

Dear Abstinens
Taking a Wife, I am told, will Save me from the
Consequences of Drink; but I am far from Convinced.
Are there Eminent Authorities who Endorse this View?
Edging to the Altar, Enfield

Dear Edging
I fear that most Authorities hold the Opposite Opinion.

The Reverend Moister writes, for example, of two
Criminals executed in Edinburgh. 'Both attributed their
Ruin to Strong Drink; but, standing on the Scaffold,
they persisted in considering *the Bad Conduct of their
Wives* as the Primary Cause of their Awful End.'[28]

You may find, Sir, that Marriage, Alcohol, and even
its Subsequent Horrors, are not as far apart as you
would Wish.

Abstinens

13

THE AWFUL EFFECTS
OF ALCOHOL

SCULLERY MAID GRAZES ON POPPIES – DISADVANTAGE OF
DRINKING ACID IN BATH WATER – VICAR'S WIFE SHOWS
CONGESTION OF BRAIN – DRUNKEN BUTLER'S
EXTRAORDINARY GAIT – HUSBAND INSENSIBLE TO NEEDLES
THRUST IN ARM – MOTHER BOOMS LIKE GUN – MAN
MANGLED ON PICNIC – RUM BLACKENS AND PUTREFIES
IMMODERATE SAILOR

Dear Abstinens
My Scullery Maid now grazes through the Garden, eating
the Poppies, which she washes down with Bath Water and
Hydrochloric Acid intended for the Drains. I fear she is
Unsuited to her Post; but wonder if you have any advice for
the unfortunate girl, before I send her on her way?
Lady H.C., Plymouth

'My Scullery Maid is Unsuited to her Post'

49

Dear Lady

What you see in your Maid is the result of the drink craving.

Dr Starke writes of inebriates 'who regularly consumed Hydrochloric Acid, Scrubbs' Ammonia, Paraffin, Carbolic Tooth Powder and bath water. Yet another Unfortunate could not wait to sit down at Table before seizing and Draining one or two Glasses of green Poppyheads.'[36]

Try persuading the girl that her Health would be helped if she drank her Bath Water in the usual fashion, unmixed with Acid.

Abstinens

Dear Abstinens

I suspect that my Wife has been Secretly Drinking. As one with no experience of Alcohol, how should I confirm this Suspicion?

Reverend W.S., Rotherhithe

Dear Reverend

The effects of Alcohol on the Brain, writes Mr Edwards, 'are Congestion, Inflammation, Epilepsy, Apoplexy, Paralysis, Softening, Delirium Tremens, Idiocy and Insanity'.[13]

Unless your Wife is in remarkably bad shape, Sir, you should be able to tell whether or not she is Drinking.

Abstinens

Dear Abstinens

My Mother, usually a quiet but steady Drinker, has become Abnormally Noisy. She now Whistles, Chimes, or Booms like a Gun, and the Neighbours – always nervous in disposition – are starting to Complain.

Surely this is not what one looks for in an elderly Lady?

Tintinnabulation, West Torrington

Dear Tintin

What you describe, though Alarming, is not the least Unusual.

According to Dr Cutten, the Drunkard has 'special and extraordinary Sounds, such as Buzzing, or a Rushing wind, Singing, Humming, Booming like a Distant Gun, Chiming like Half-heard Bells, Whistling and Muttering'.[6]

Perhaps some Compromise is possible, such as persuading your Mother to Chime on the Hour?

Abstinens

*'My mother now
Booms like a Gun'*

Dear Abstinens

Our Butler has developed a curious Way of Walking. He lifts his Foot high in the Air, bringing it down noisily on the Heel, then balancing momentarily on his Toes; after which, he Repeats the Operation.

As you may imagine, this is more than a little Disturbing at a Dinner Party.

Lieutenant-Colonel B.M.R.S, Suffolk

Dear Lieutenant-Colonel

What you are witnessing, Sir, is a Habitual Drunkard. His gait, writes Dr Archdall Reid, 'is as though he were stepping over some Object in his path. The Foot is thrown forward and the Toe lifted high; the Heel is brought down first, and then the rest of the Foot.'[35]

51

Before your next Dinner, Colonel, you would be well advised to see what remains of your Cellar.

Abstinens

Dear Abstinens
It is increasingly hard to gain my Husband's attention. He sits staring in front of him, holding his Porter, and seems not to feel the Candle Flame I hold to his Head, or the needles I sometimes insert in his Arm.

Formerly, either of these Methods would attract him immediately.

Worried Wife, Upper Warlingham

Dear Worried
Clearly the Porter is taking its Effect.

The Imbiber, says Mr Barnett, 'lacks control of the Muscles of Locomotion. There is insensibility to feeling of Pain, and ignorance of sensation, *such as Needle-Thrusts.*'[2]

Have you thought, dear Lady, of using longer Needles; or else of leaving your Husband to sup uninterrupted?

Abstinens

'Have you thought of using longer Needles?'

Dear Abstinens
My Betrothed plans a River Picnic, and wishes to take Wine,
as well as the usual Comestibles.

Do you suppose it safe to mix Water and Wine in this
fashion?

Always Cautious, Mansfield

Dear Cautious
You are right to be concerned. Consider the sad fate of
James Crawley and his wife, *both intoxicated on a Picnic,*
'who laid down near the river's bank at Niagara Falls.
The next morning, the man's mangled Remains were
found on the rock one hundred and fifty feet below, *and*
the woman caught in a Tree, ten feet over the bank.'[15]

Abstinens

Dear Abstinens
I have noticed that my Father turns a Tenebrous Shade when
refreshing himself with new rum; which, I am afraid, he does
more than he should. Further, Father now has a curious
odour.

Can you tell what Action I should take?

Devoted Daughter, Brighton

Dear Devoted
You omit to mention whether your Father is still Alive?

Mr Morewood recounts the case of a Seaman in the
West Indies 'who drank a quart of New Rum, died
suddenly, turned quite Black in several parts of his
body, and was evidently in a putrescent state.'[29]

If this is, indeed, your Parent's condition, it is not
unfilial to admit that there is little more you can do for
him.

Abstinens

14

THE DRINKING DRIVER

Dear Abstinens
Being a Commerical Traveller (Razor Strops and Sundry
Articles) I drive many Miles a Month. I also take what we in
the Trade term a Liquid Lunch. This last week, however, I
have been cautioned by a Constable that a man should not
Drink and Drive.

What do the Experts have to say on this Subject?

Open Road, currently of Kent

Dear Open
Here Dr Ridge – to name but one – is fixed in his
Opinion. Alcohol, he affirms, is a great Distraction to
the Driver. *'It makes him take less notice of the Horse,*
which thus can start off Dangerously Quickly, and
thereafter Follow its own Course.'[36]

You will sell very few Strops, Sir, should the
Constabulary apprehend you driving Drunk in charge of
your Beast.

Abstinens

'Alcohol makes him
take less notice
of the Horse'

15

BODILY DISSOLUTION

RELIGION AND INTEMPERANCE TOLD BY TEETH –
AFFLICTED COAL-WHIPPER DIES DIRECTLY – CHOLERA
PREFERABLE TO ALCOHOL – DOES NOT MAKE MAN INTO
ANIMAL

Dear Abstinens
I have often wondered whether a man's Religion can be told
by his Teeth.
    Is this possible, or are the Jaws generally unaffected by our
Choice of Worship?

Ecumenical Observer, Epsom Downs

Dear Ecumenical
On the contrary, the Teeth are Excellent Indicators of
their owner's Inclinations and Habits. Sir Thomas
Barlow relates that 'from the teeth of three hundred and
ninety-eight Mohammedan labourers, *he was able to tell*
at once whether they had remained Faithful to the Prophet,
or whether they had been Seduced into European habits
of Drink'.[1]

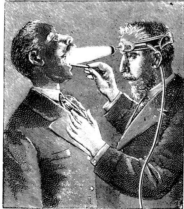

Abstinens

'the Teeth are Excellent Indicators of their owner's Inclinations'

Dear Abstinens
As a Coal-Whipper, long committed to the Bottle, I have been told that my Life is worth Very Little.

What chance do you suppose I have of Extending my Earthly Span?

Worried Whipper, Acton West

Dear Worried
To be Frank with you, your Days are Numbered. According to the Reverend William Moister (who should know) 'the mortality among Coal-Whippers who are brought to London hospitals is Frightful. The moment these Beer Drinkers are attacked with Acute Disease, they Die directly.'[28]

Your best Advice, Sir, is to Prepare your Soul for a world in which you will Whip no more Coal.

Abstinens

Dear Abstinens
I fear that my Husband, who goes persistently to the Gin Palace, will catch the Cholera now rife there.

In these Unhappy Circumstances, how should I protect him?

Mother of Seven, Maidstone

Dear Mother
You should consider the Cholera a Blessed Relief. Cholera, writes Dr Ridge, 'would never do so much harm as Alcohol; it would never make men Animals; nor cause them to Lose their Souls'.[36]

Consider the Cholera, dear Lady, as Nature's Way of turning your Husband teetotal.

Abstinens

16

ALCOHOL AND YOUR PET

DRINKING TERRIER NOW NEEDS NIGHT-LIGHT –
GUINEA-PIG UNWISE TO DRINK IF PREGNANT – LAMB FALLS
INTO ALCOHOLIC COMPANY – ALCOHOL NOT GOOD FOR
JELLYFISH

Dear Abstinens
I have this dog, it is mainly a Jack Russell Terrier, it is
partial to Beer with its Meat. It has had half a pint of Bitter
regular, since a Puppy. The problem being, it is now Noisy of
an evening, and will not rest without it has a Night-Light. Is
this usual in a drinking Dog?

Sleepless Hours, Hackney

Dear Sleepless
What you describe is a common condition of the
inebriate animal. Dr Magnan of Paris has spent many
years in studying the subject. He observes that a
drinking dog 'cries and whines plaintively, and cannot
be reassured by its master's voice; frequently it is
necessary to bring a light into the room before it can be
quieted'.[19]

Your Terrier may, of course, simply be Unsuited to
Alcohol. There are many Dogs that take nothing
stronger than Milk.

Abstinens

'it is partial to Beer with its Meat'

Dear Abstinens
Following your Advice on the Alcoholic Dog, I am writing to
ask whether my Guinea-Pig should also Abstain?
Worried Animal Lover, West Hoathly

Dear Worried
You do not mention the Sex of your Pet; but it should
definitely not be Drinking if it is a Female, or Pregnant.
Dr Fere has noted that with Guinea-Pigs 'subjected to
the continuous use of Alcohol during Pregnancy,
morbid Changes are found in the Brain of the
Offspring'.[19]

   Believe me, a litter of Unintelligent and Intemperate
Guinea-Pigs is Something to Avoid.

Abstinens

Dear Abstinens
Recently two Lambs have been setting a Poor Example to the
rest of the Flock, in attempting to Mount each other. By the
usual standards of Lambs, these Animals are undoubtedly
Delinquent.
   Might Alcohol make them behave in this way?
Mutton Dressed as Lamb, East Malling

Dear Mutton
Your Lambs may well have fallen into bad company. Mr
Morewood records the case of a South African lamb,
fortunately white, 'whose great love is for draught beer.
It will lift the can up with its Front Paws and drink with
such relish that it can at once be seen *it has been Led
Away by a very Bad Example*.'[29]

Abstinens

Dear Abstinens

Since the last Works Outing to Eastbourne, I have kept a small Jellyfish, it is mainly for Companionship.

Now the Ice is Broken, I have grown close to this Fish; but it has recently been Out of Sorts. Would Alcohol improve its condition?

Fruit of the Sea, Frinton

Dear Fruit

Alcohol will do your Jellyfish no good at all. Sir B.W. Richardson, MD records that his own Jellyfish was swimming 'seventy-four to the minute' until Alcohol was added to its Water. Then, he writes, these movements stopped. 'The animal began to shrink and sink to the bottom of the vessel. At the end of five minutes the little Creature lay at the bottom, apparently Dead.'[19]

Sir B.W. Richardson's Jellyfish never again swam at seventy-four to the minute. Indeed, it has not swum at all.

You should find some other way of Cheering your Pet.   Abstinens

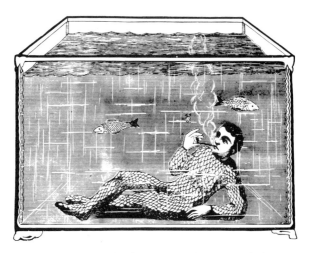

'I have kept a small Jellyfish . . . mainly for companionship'

17

THE TOTAL ABSTAINER

FELT HATS AND PRESERVATION OF BODIES AMONG
PERMISSIBLE USES OF ALCOHOL – LIQUOR USED TO
PRESERVE REMAINS OF FATHER-IN-LAW – SAILORS DRINK
DEAD ADMIRAL DRY

Dear Abstinens
My Wife and I have recently renounced the Demon Drink.
However, we are reluctant to waste the Liquor accumulated
in many years of Sinful Insobriety.
  Are there any Permissible uses for Alcohol?
                            Road to Damascus, Redhill

Dear Road
According to Mr Edwards, 'the acceptable uses of
Alcohol are for Burial Caskets; Dental Goods; Fuel;
Hats, both Straw and Felt; Preservation of Bodies; and
Quick-drying Paint'.[11]

                            Abstinens

Dear Abstinens
Following your Advice, we have decided to use our remaining
Liquor to preserve the Body of my Wife's Father, recently
Deceased.
  Can you Inform us how long we may expect to Maintain
him in this way?
                            Road to Damascus, Redhill

Dear Road
Much depends on whether your entire Family has taken
the Pledge.
  Mr Delavan records the sad case of an Admiral who

died at sea, 'and was put in a Rum Puncheon to
Preserve him. But sailors tapped the Cask and drank his
Liquor, leaving the Admiral high and dry.'[7]

Of course, if all the Family refrain from Drinking
your Father-in-Law, he should last some time.

Abstinens

*'we have to decided to use
our remaining Liquor to
preserve the Body of my
Wife's Father'*

18

TREATING THE TOPER

DIPSOMANIAC KNIGHT DOUSES ROSES IN CARPET –
ADVISABLE TO TICKLE THROAT BEFORE THRASHING WIFE –
SOAP-AND-WATER ENEMA COMPLETES TREATMENT – LET
DRUNKARD DIE TO LEAD MORE MANLY LIFE

Dear Abstinens
My Husband has recently taken to rinsing the Roses on our
Carpet. Meanwhile, he tells me to keep Calm.
I am, of course, perfectly calm. But I wonder whether Sir
Joshua might be Drinking a Little?
                              The Hon. Mrs Adelaide R. S., Wantage

Dear Honorable
Possibly more than a little. According to Dr Frederick
Heman Hubbard, 'the patient who rushes into his
parlours and dashes Bucketsful of water over Red Spots
in the Carpet, which he mistakes for a Fire, at the same
time giving his wife the Suggestive Advice not to get
Excited' – this man, says Dr Heman Hubbard, 'presents
an early phase of the Dipsomaniac's malady'.[4]
   The cure is that recommended by the classical author
Pliny: 'a Lion's stercus, or wine in which an Eel has
been suffocated'.

                                                        Abstinens

Dear Abstinens
Thank you for the Cure of Dipsomania. I am Anxious to try
it, as the White Lodge is now awash with Water.
*   However, our Butcher, though a pleasant enough fellow,*
has never heard of a Lion's stercus. Nor have I yet succeeded
in Suffocating an Eel.

Should I perhaps Lift the Carpet?
The Hon. Mrs Adelaide R.S., Wantage

Dear Honorable
Lifting the Carpet is no Answer; one wants to cure Sir Joshua completely. If you have given up the Lion, persevere with the Eel.

Admittedly, drowning a Fish is not the Nicest of Tasks; but many women write to say they are glad to have taken the Trouble.

Few things put people off their Wine like finding an Eel suffocated in it.

Abstinens

Dear Abstinens
My Wife, I fear, regularly Surfeits herself with Alcohol. I have been advised to thrash her with Wet Towels. Is this, I wonder, a generally recognised way of treating the Inebriate Woman?

In Sickness and in Health, Surrey

Dear Sickness
Simply thrashing your Wife with a Towel is unlikely to do the trick. Mr Wishart recommends first Tickling the back of the Throat with a Feather. Only then should you Thrash the Afflicted with Cold, Wet Towels; and complete the Treatment by pouring Cold Water all over her.[42]

To this cure, Dr Heman Hubbard suggests adding 'a large Soap-and-Water Enema, thoroughly to wash out the lower Bowels'.[21]

You may well find, after the first few nights, that your Wife will wish to do without her evening tipple.

Abstinens

Dear Abstinens
I have a close Cousin who is now much Reduced by Drink.
He seems unlikely to be much Longer for this World.
  How should I best Prolong my Relation's Life?
                                    Careworn, Caterham

Dear Careworn
If you follow the Reverend Jeffrey's advice, you will let
your Relative go Quietly Hence.

'Let the Drunkard die,' writes Reverend Jeffreys, 'if
die he must, Struggling and fighting his way onward to a
Manlier Life, encouraged in the Faith that his efforts
will receive no check by that form of Death, but will
continue on, under more Favourable Circumstances, in
Another Life.'[23]

Your Cousin, of course, may take some time to
appreciate this new Perspective.

                                    Abstinens

'his Efforts will continue on, under more Favourable Circumstances'